PIANO/VOCAL    SELECTIONS FROM THE MOVIE

BOUBLIL AND SCHÖNBERG'S

# Les Misérables

# OUR JOURNEY IN MOVIELAND

From the start we knew that the stage version would not make a film and that changes would be needed. At the theatre, the curtain rises on a world suggested by the set, the overture, and the convention of singing, which is where the evening's journey begins. We are, at first, distant spectators of what unfolds, until we hopefully warm towards the plot and the songs. Lighting, set, and staging direct our attention to where it should focus.

In a film, the camera is our eyes and cuts right to the heart of the action, sharing now and then, in close-up, the flicker of a smile or a trembling hand. At the cinema, the actors do not project towards the auditorium as in a theatre, so the behaviour, and thus the words, have to be delivered differently. No set changes on the big screen, no theatrical coup like the opening of the Barricade. The links are as short as you wish, and the effects that you can imagine in a screenplay are limitless.

All these thoughts inspired the screenplay, which we co-wrote with William Nicholson and Herbert Kretzmer, several new scenes drawn from Victor Hugo's novel, which were finally able to find their place, and a completely new song, "Suddenly," created for Hugh Jackman, whose voice was a blessing to its creation. We also discovered how Anne Hathaway, Russell Crowe, Amanda Seyfried, Eddie Redmayne, Sacha Baron Cohen, Helena Bonham Carter, Samantha Barks, and Aaron Tveit could re-shape the songs that we thought we knew and make them their own.

All of this compelled us to reconsider our score, its construction, its orchestrations, the necessary interstitial dialogue during a long process. Little by little, the new version took shape in close collaboration with Tom Hooper, Cameron Mackintosh, and the Working Title Films team, including producers Eric Fellner, Tim Bevan and Debra Hayward. Our objective was to protect the spontaneity of the drama and the unity of the musical work at the same time and reinvent it as if it had been written this way in the beginning. Add to that the challenge of putting down the live recording of actors and making the orchestrations *after* shooting, and you have a picture of how exciting the journey has been.

This movie selections song book contains 16 songs: many favourites, some in slightly different forms, two with new sections added for the movie, including a Gavroche section in "Look Down," back from the 1980 original French show, and one brand new song, "Suddenly,"— written especially for Jean Valjean/Hugh Jackman, for the scene after he discovers the strength of his new fatherly feeling for little Cosette— which aims to capture Victor Hugo's beautiful statements about how two unhappy souls can make one happy human being.

*Alain Boublil and Claude-Michel Schönberg*
December 2012

# Les Misérables

Screenplay by
William Nicholson
Alain Boublil and Claude-Michel Schönberg
Herbert Kretzmer

Music by
Claude-Michel Schönberg

Lyrics by
Herbert Kretzmer

Original French text by
Alain Boublil
and Jean-Marc Natel

Based on the original stage musical
Boublil and Schönberg's
*Les Misérables*
From the novel by Victor Hugo
Produced on stage by Cameron Mackintosh

Hugh Jackman             Russell Crowe
Anne Hathaway            Amanda Seyfried

Eddie Redmayne       Aaron Tveit       Samantha Barks
Isabelle Allen      Daniel Huttlestone      Colm Wilkinson

with
Helena Bonham Carter and Sacha Baron Cohen

Directed by
Tom Hooper

Produced by
Tim Bevan, Eric Fellner, and Debra Hayward

Produced by
Cameron Mackintosh

FIGHT. DREAM. HOPE. LOVE.

# AT THE END OF THE DAY

Music by CLAUDE-MICHEL SCHÖNBERG
Lyrics by ALAIN BOUBLIL, JEAN-MARC NATEL
and HERBERT KRETZMER

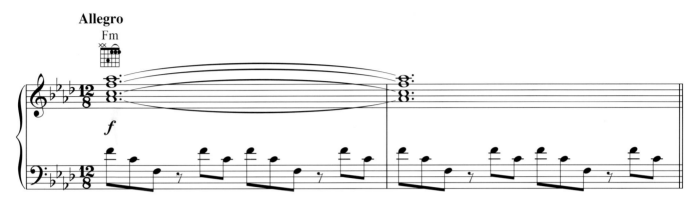

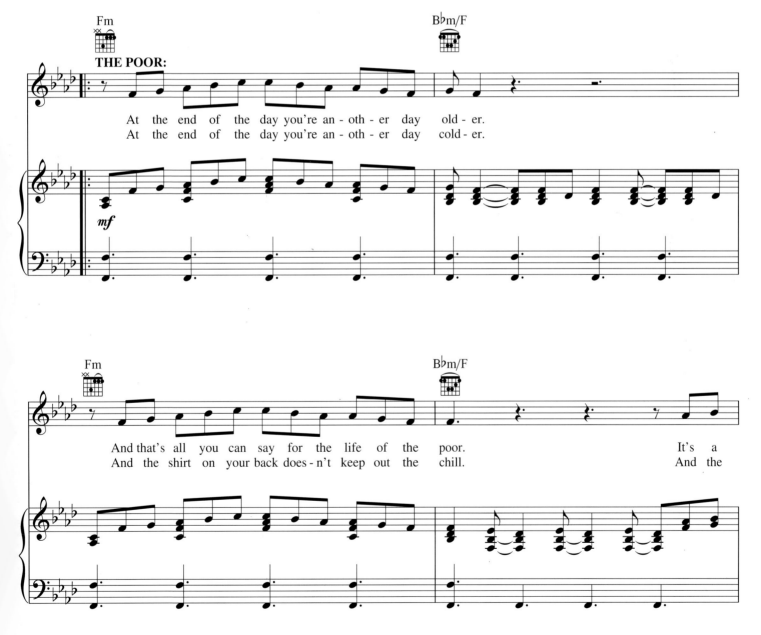

**THE POOR:**

At the end of the day you're an-oth-er day old-er.
At the end of the day you're an-oth-er day cold-er.

And that's all you can say for the life of the poor. It's a
And the shirt on your back does-n't keep out the chill. And the

struggle, __ it's a war. And there's noth-ing that an-y-one's giv-ing. One more
right-eous __ hur-ry past. They don't hear the lit-tle ones cry-ing. And the

day stand - ing a - bout, what is it for?
win-ter is com-ing on fast, read - y to kill.

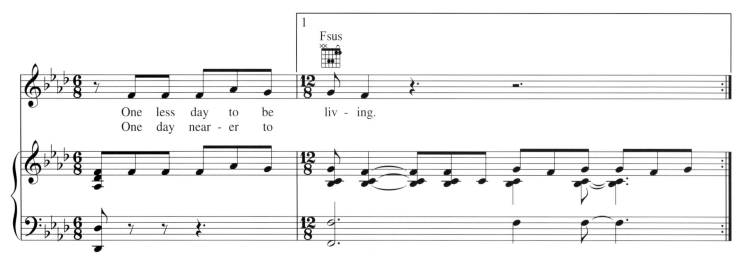

One less day to be liv - ing.
One day near - er to

dy - ing.

THE WORKERS:

At the end of the day there's an - oth - er day
At the end of the day it's an - oth - er day

dawn - ing.
o - ver,

And the sun in the morn-ing is wait-ing to
with e - nough in your pock - et to last for a

rise.
week.

Like the waves crash _ on the sand, like a
Pay the land - lord, _ pay the shop. Keep on

storm that -'ll break an - y sec - ond, there's a hun - ger _ in the land. There's a
graft - ing as long as you're a - ble. Keep on graft - ing _ till you drop, or it's

reck - on - ing still to be reck - oned. And there's gon - na be hell _ to
back to the crumbs off the ta - ble. Well, you've got to pay _ your

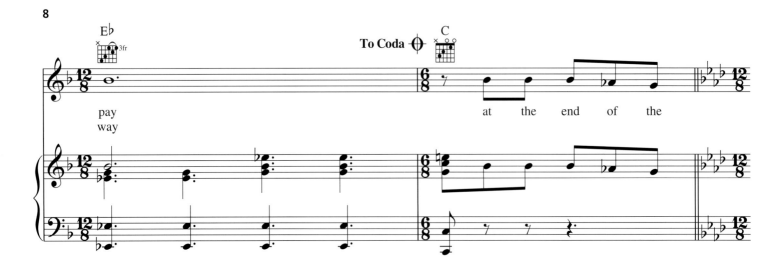

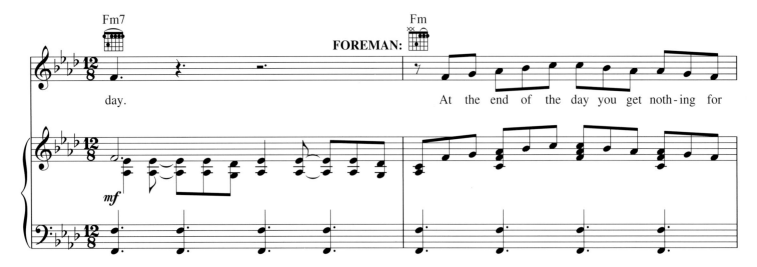

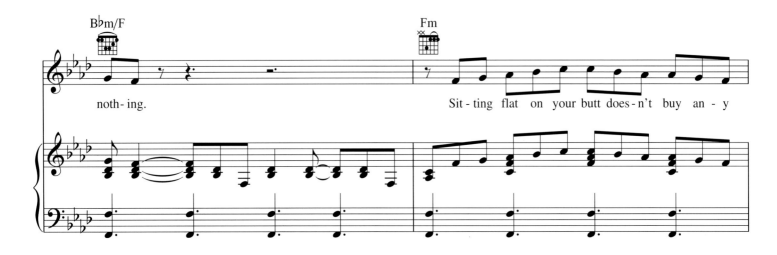

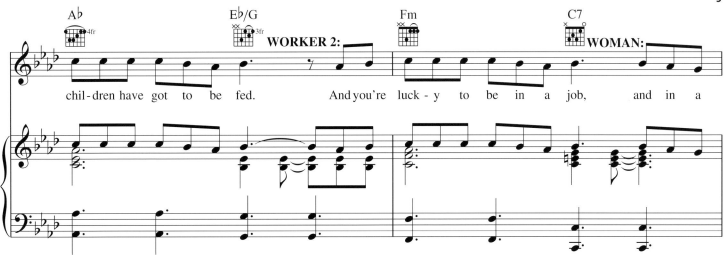

chil-dren have got to be fed. And you're luck-y to be in a job, and in a

WORKER 2:

WOMAN:

bed.

ALL:

And we're count-ing our

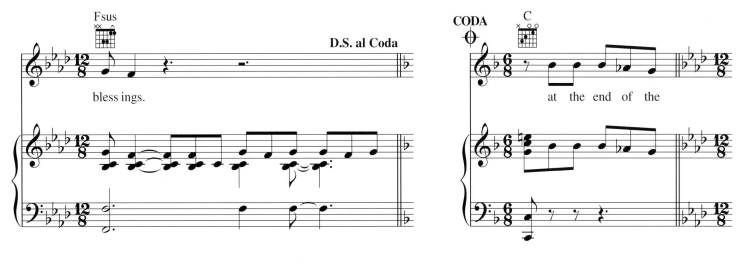

bless ings.

D.S. al Coda

CODA

at the end of the

day.

# I DREAMED A DREAM

Music by CLAUDE-MICHEL SCHÖNBERG
Lyrics by ALAIN BOUBLIL, JEAN-MARC NATEL
and HERBERT KRETZMER

**Andante**

FANTINE:

I dreamed a dream in days gone by, when hope was high and life worth liv- ing. I dreamed that love would nev- er die. I dreamed that God would be for- giv- ing. Then I was young and un- a-

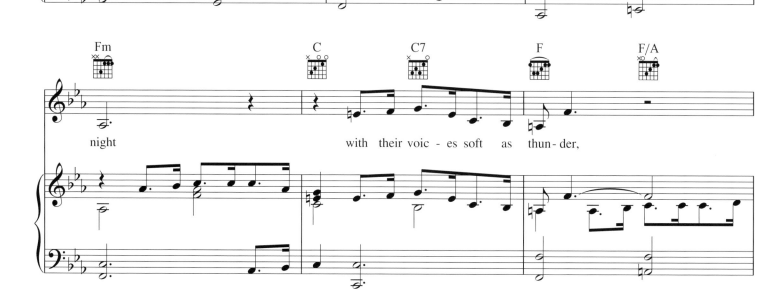

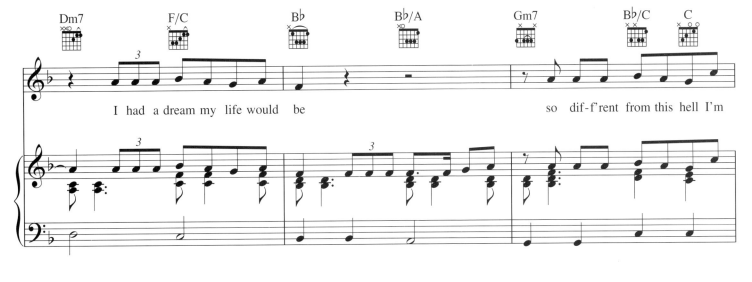

I had a dream my life would be so dif-f'rent from this hell I'm

liv - ing, ____ so dif-f'rent now from what it seemed.

Now life has killed the dream I dreamed.

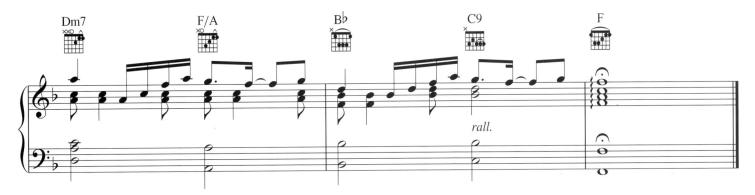

# I HAVE A CRIME TO DECLARE

Music by CLAUDE-MICHEL SCHÖNBERG
Lyrics by HERBERT KRETZMER and ALAIN BOUBLIL

You say this man is going to trial and that he's sure to be re - turned to serve his

*cresc.*

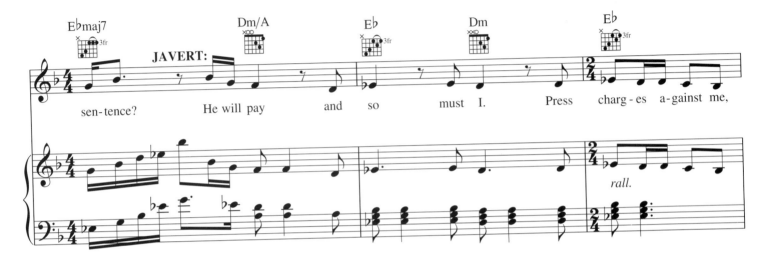

**JAVERT:**

sen - tence? He will pay and so must I. Press charg - es a - gainst me,

*rall.*

**VALJEAN:**

sir! You have on - ly done your du - ty. It's a mi - nor sin, at most. All of

*p a tempo*   *mf*

**JAVERT:**   **VALJEAN:**

us have been mis-tak- en. You'll re - turn, sir, to your post. Must I do as you say? It's your du - ty to o-bey.

*rit.*

# WHO AM I?

right
Music by CLAUDE-MICHEL SCHÖNBERG
Lyrics by ALAIN BOUBLIL, JEAN-MARC NATEL
and HERBERT KRETZMER

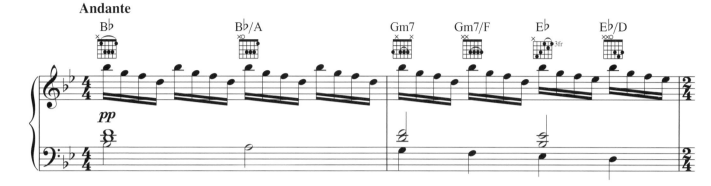

20

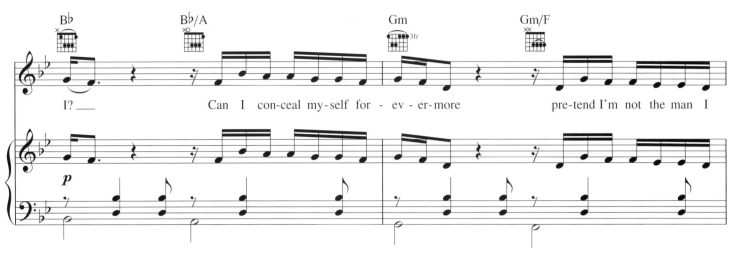

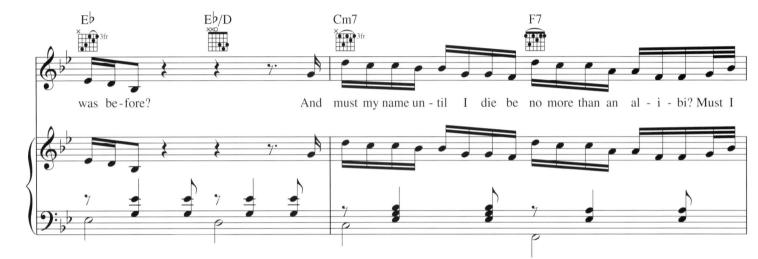

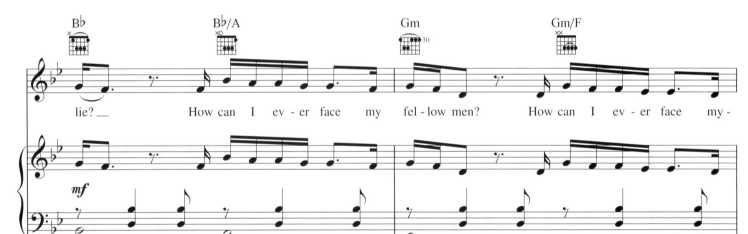

# CASTLE ON A CLOUD

Music by CLAUDE-MICHEL SCHÖNBERG
Lyrics by ALAIN BOUBLIL, JEAN-MARC NATEL
and HERBERT KRETZMER

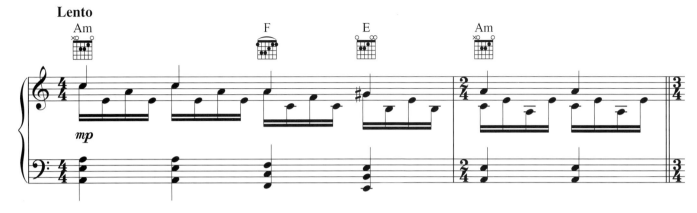

There is a cas - tle on a cloud.
There is a room that's full of toys.

I like to go there in my sleep.
There are a hun - dred boys and girls.

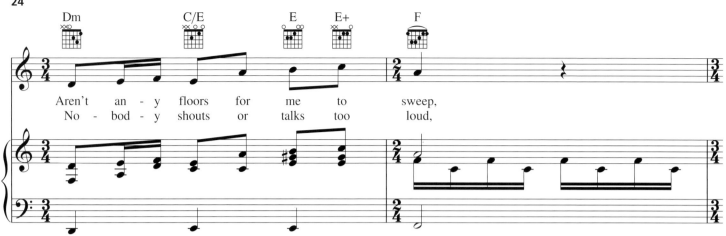

Aren't an - y floors for me to sweep,
No - bod - y shouts or talks too loud,

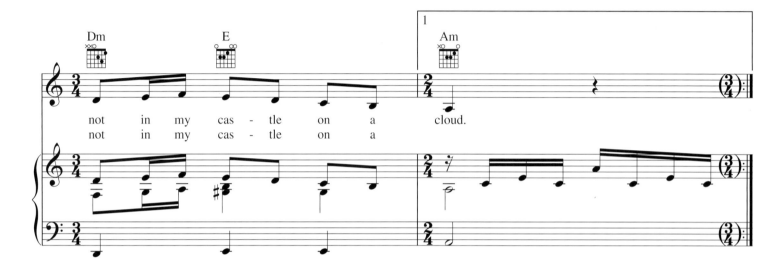

not in my cas - tle on a cloud.
not in my cas - tle on a

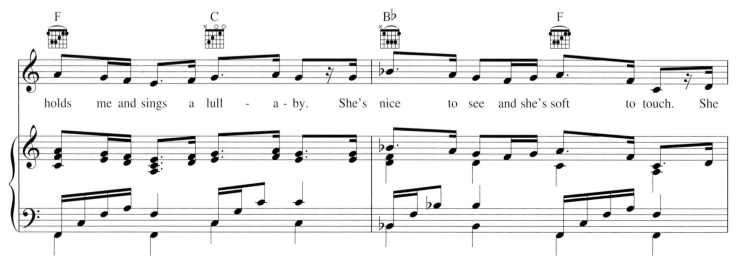

cloud. There is a la - dy all in white, ___

holds me and sings a lull - a - by. She's nice to see and she's soft to touch. She

says, "Co - sette, I love you ver - y much." I know a place where no one's

lost. I know a place where no one cries.

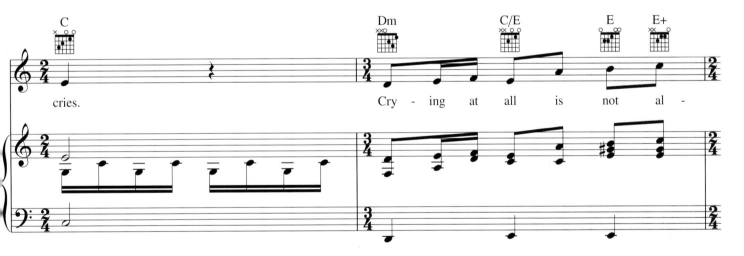

cries. Cry - ing at all is not al -

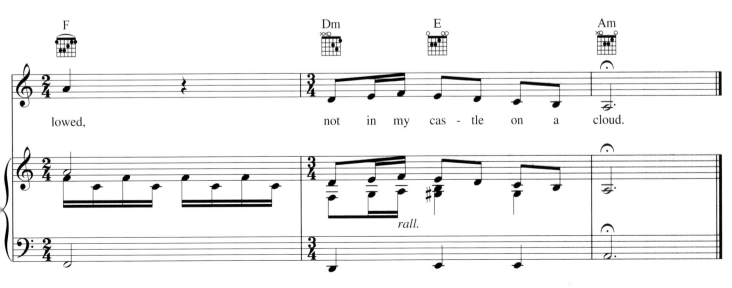

lowed, not in my cas - tle on a cloud.

# MASTER OF THE HOUSE

Music by CLAUDE–MICHEL SCHÖNBERG
Lyrics by ALAIN BOUBLIL, JEAN-MARC NATEL
and HERBERT KRETZMER

hon - est men like me, a gent of good in - tent who's con -

tent to be... Mas - ter of the house,
Food be - yond com - pare,

dol - ing out the charm ready - y with a hand-shake and an o - pen palm.
food be - yond be - lief, mix it in a min - cer and pre - tend it's beef.

Tells a sauc - y tale, makes a lit - tle stir, cus - tom - ers ap - pre - ci - ate a
Kid - ney of a horse, liv - er of a cat, fill - ing up the sau - sag - es with

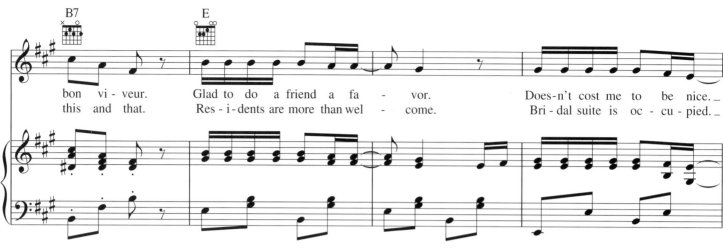

bon vi - veur.    Glad to do a friend a fa - vor.    Does-n't cost me to be nice. _
this and that.    Res - i - dents are more than wel - come.    Bri - dal suite is oc - cu - pied. _

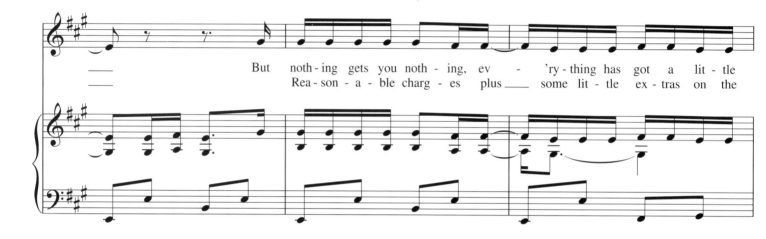

_ But noth - ing gets you noth - ing, ev - 'ry - thing has got a lit - tle
_ Rea - son - a - ble charg - es plus _ some lit - tle ex - tras on the

price. _    Mas - ter of the house,    keep - er of the zoo,
side. _    Charge 'em for the lice,    ex - tra for the mice,

read - y to re - lieve them of a sou or two.    Wa - ter - ing the wine,
two per - cent for look - ing in the mir - ror twice.    Here a lit - tle slice,

# SUDDENLY

Music by CLAUDE-MICHEL SCHÖNBERG
Lyrics by HERBERT KRETZMER and ALAIN BOUBLIL

# STARS

Music by CLAUDE-MICHEL SCHÖNBERG
Lyrics by HERBERT KRETZMER and ALAIN BOUBLIL

# LOOK DOWN
## (Gavroche/Éponine new sections)

Music by CLAUDE-MICHEL SCHÖNBERG
Lyrics by ALAIN BOUBLIL, JEAN-MARC NATEL
and HERBERT KRETZMER

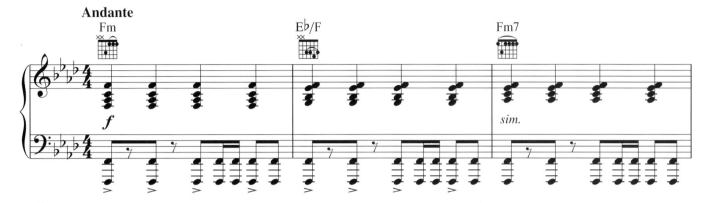

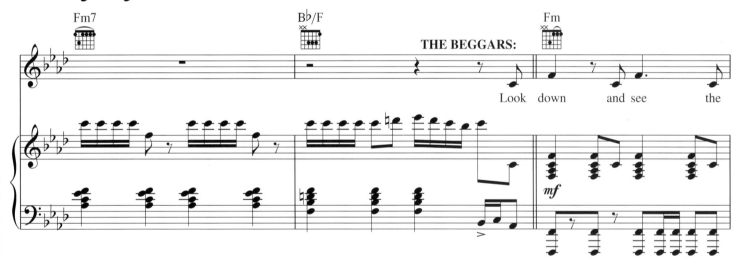

**THE BEGGARS:**

Look down and see the

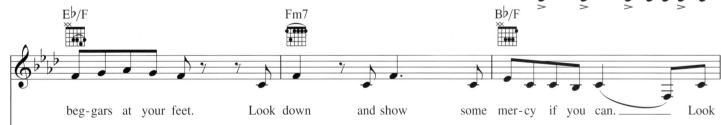

beg-gars at your feet. Look down and show some mer-cy if you can. _____ Look

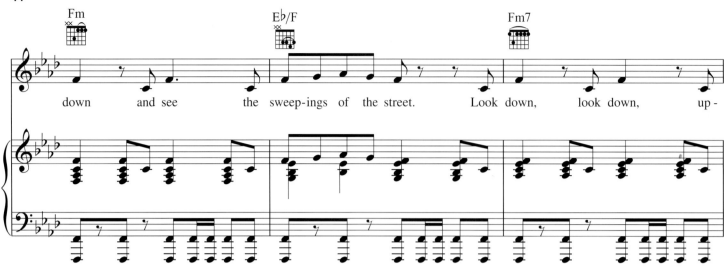

down and see the sweep-ings of the street. Look down, look down, up-

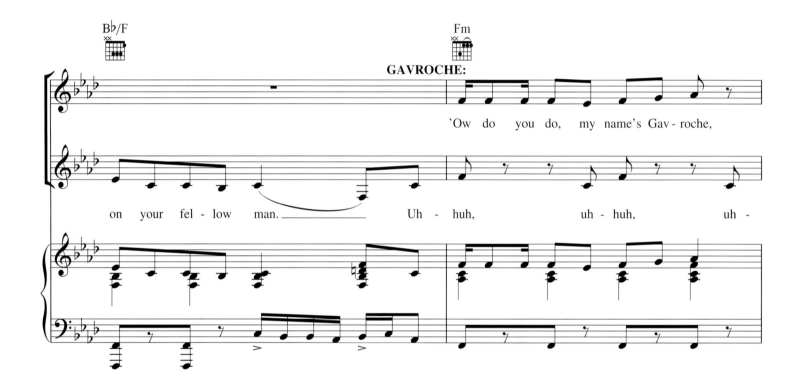

**GAVROCHE:**

'Ow do you do, my name's Gav - roche,

on your fel - low man. _____ Uh - huh, uh - huh, uh -

These are my peo - ple, here's my patch. Not much to look at, noth - ing posh,

huh _____ Uh - huh, uh - huh, uh -

**B♭/F** — noth-ing that you'd call up to scratch. **A♭** — This is my school, my high so - ci - e - ty,

huh _____ Uh - huh, uh - huh, uh -

**E♭** — here in the slums of St. Mi - chel. **G♭** — We live on crumbs of hum - ble pi - e - ty,

huh, uh - huh, uh - huh, uh - huh.

**D♭** — tough on the teeth, but what the hell. Think you're poor? Think you're free? **C5** — Fol-low me, Fol-low me! Look

**THE BEGGARS:**

*cresc.*

**ÉPONINE:**
Hey there, Mon-sieur, what's new with you? Have-n't seen much of you of late.

Plan-ning, no doubt, to change the world? Plot-ting to o-ver-throw the state?

Still liv-ing here in this old sewer? Might as well doss down in a ditch.

# DO YOU HEAR THE PEOPLE SING?

Music by CLAUDE-MICHEL SCHÖNBERG
Lyrics by ALAIN BOUBLIL, JEAN-MARC NATEL
and HERBERT KRETZMER

ENJOLRAS & STUDENTS:

Do you hear the peo- ple sing, sing-ing the

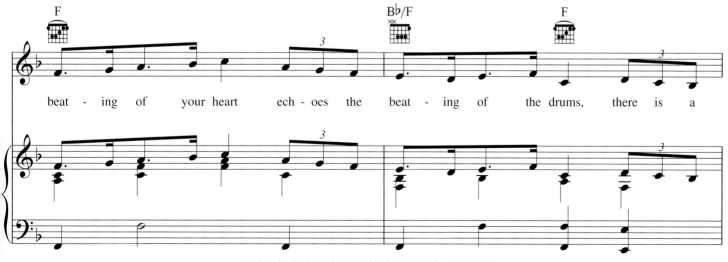

song of an- gry men? It is the mu- sic of a peo- ple who will not be slaves a-gain! When the

beat- ing of your heart ech- oes the beat- ing of the drums, there is a

song of an-gry men? It is the mu-sic of a peo-ple who will not be slaves a-gain! When the

beat-ing of yourheart ech-oes the beat-ing of the drums, there is a life a-bout to start when to-mor-row

**STUDENTS & CROWD:**

comes! Will you life a-bout to start when to-mor-row comes!

# A HEART FULL OF LOVE

Music by CLAUDE-MICHEL SCHÖNBERG
Lyrics by ALAIN BOUBLIL, JEAN-MARC NATEL
and HERBERT KRETZMER

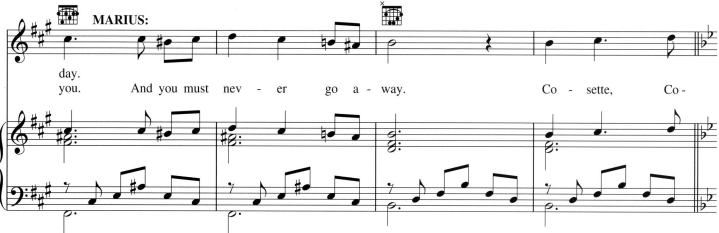

# ON MY OWN

Music by CLAUDE-MICHEL SCHÖNBERG
Lyrics by ALAIN BOUBLIL, JEAN-MARC NATEL,
HERBERT KRETZMER, JOHN CAIRD
and TREVOR NUNN

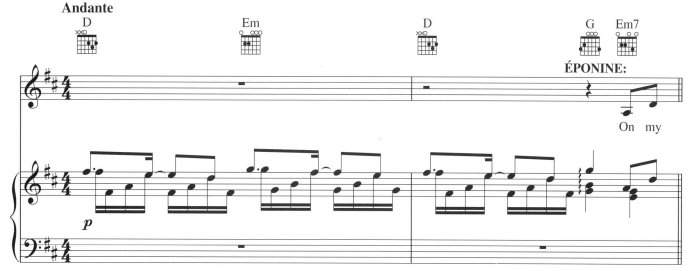

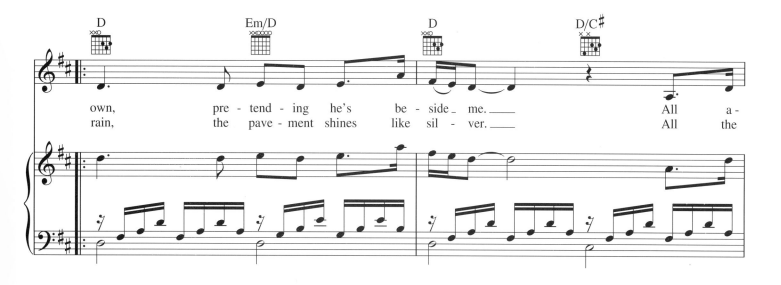

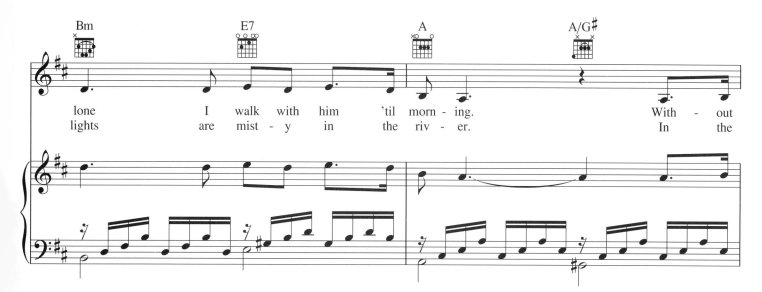

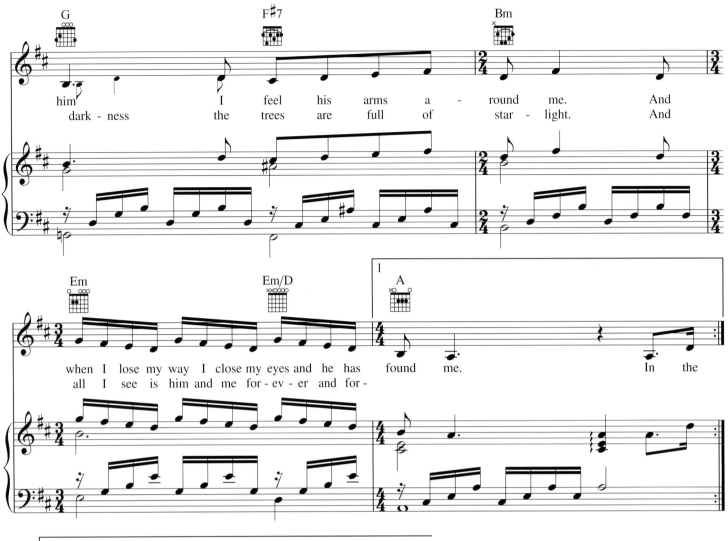

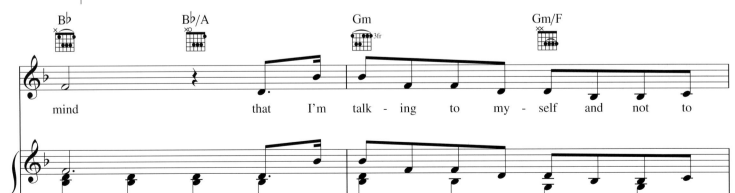

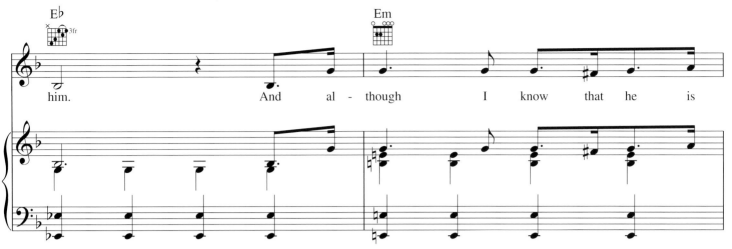

him. And al - though I know that he is

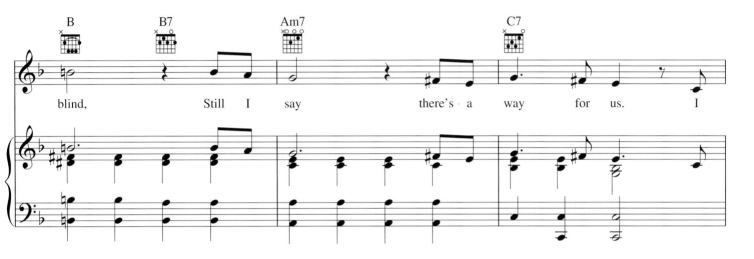

blind, Still I say there's a way for us. I

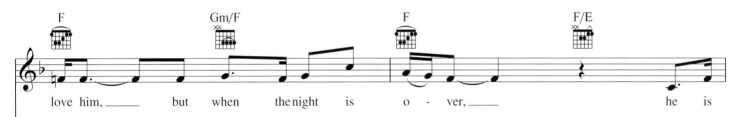

love him, _____ but when the night is o - ver, _____ he is

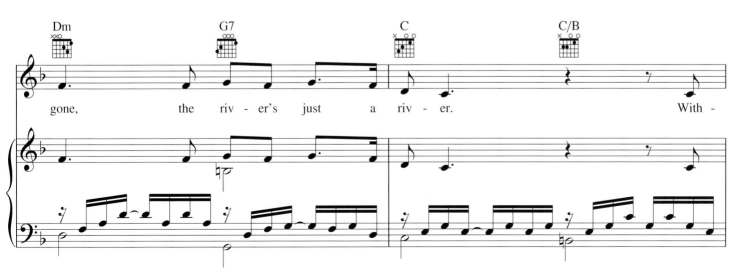

gone, the riv - er's just a riv - er. With -

out him the world a-round me chang - es. The

trees are bare and ev-'ry-where the streets are full of stran - gers. I

love him _____ but ev-'ry day I'm learn - ing _____ all my

life I've on-ly been pre-tend - ing. _____ With -

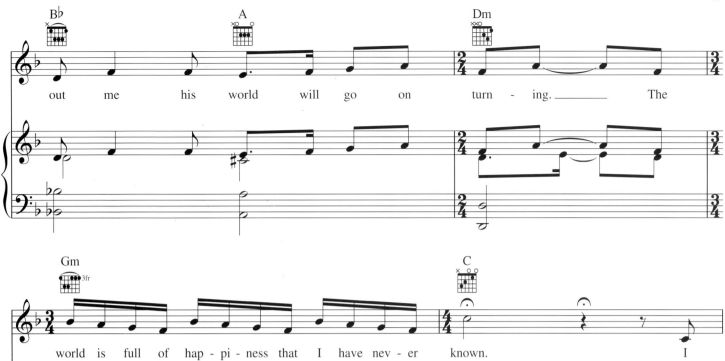

out me his world will go on turn - ing. _____ The

world is full of hap - pi - ness that I have nev - er known. I

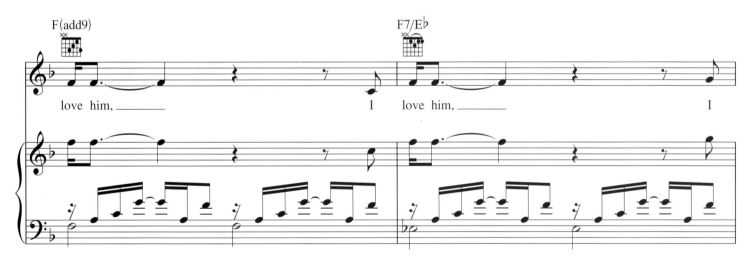

love him, _____ I love him, _____ I

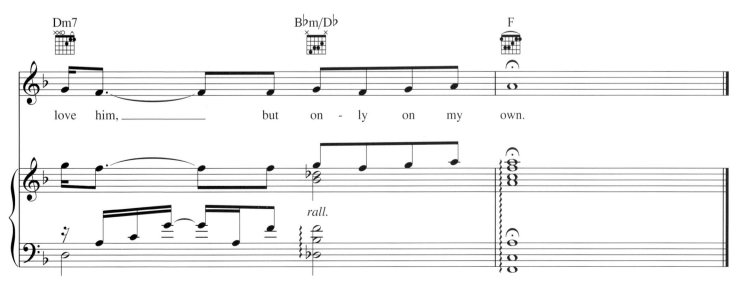

love him, _____ but on - ly on my own.

# A LITTLE FALL OF RAIN

Music by CLAUDE-MICHEL SCHÖNBERG
Lyrics by ALAIN BOUBLIL, JEAN-MARC NATEL
and HERBERT KRETZMER

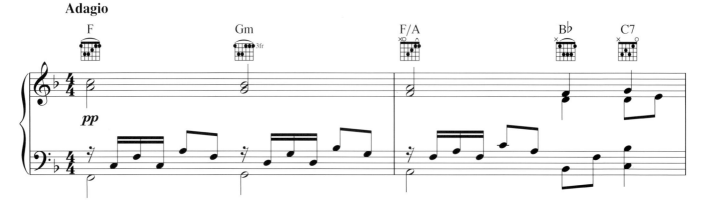

ÉPONINE:
Don't you fret, ___ M' sieur Mar - ius, ___ I don't feel an - y pain. A

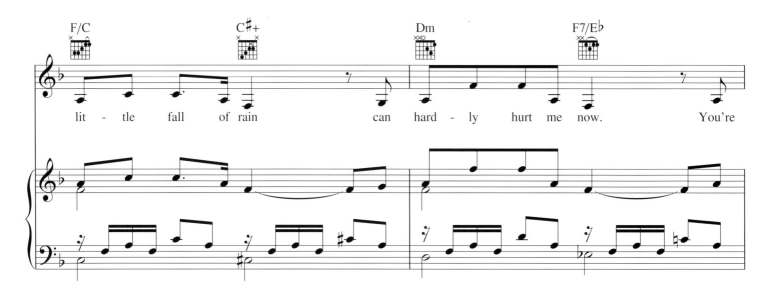

lit - tle fall of rain can hard - ly hurt me now. You're

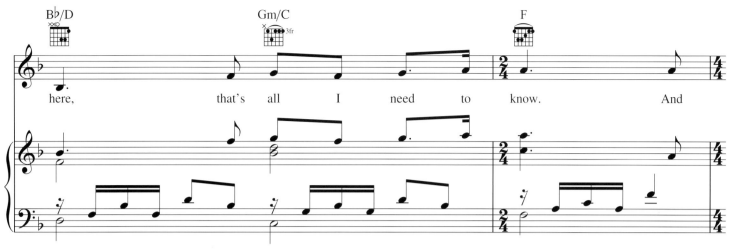

here, that's all I need to know. And

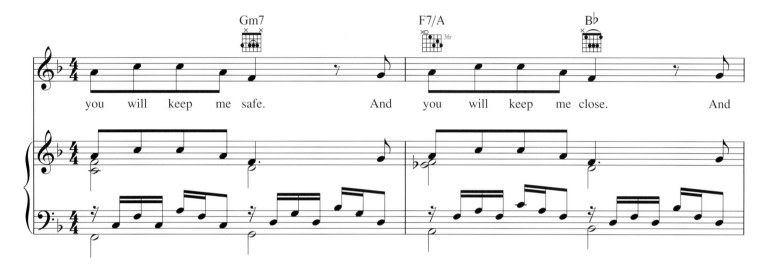

you will keep me safe. And you will keep me close. And

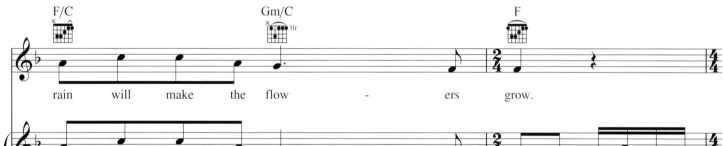

rain will make the flow - ers grow.

**MARIUS:**

But you will live, 'Pon - ine, Dear God a - bove.

If I could close your wounds with words of

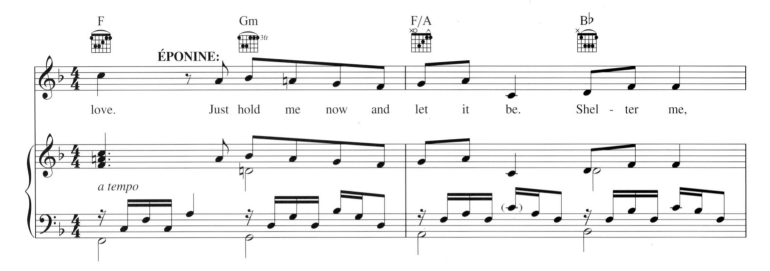

ÉPONINE:
love. Just hold me now and let it be. Shel- ter me,

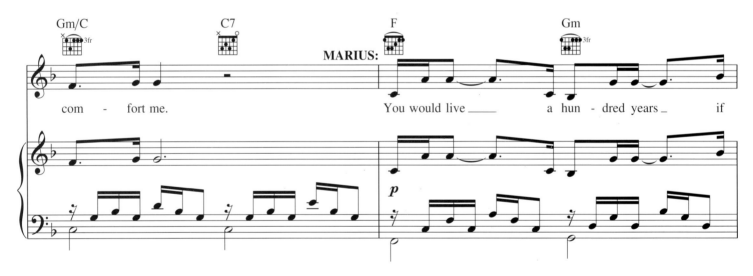

MARIUS:
com - fort me. You would live ___ a hun - dred years ___ if

ÉPONINE:
I could show you how. I won't de - sert you now. The

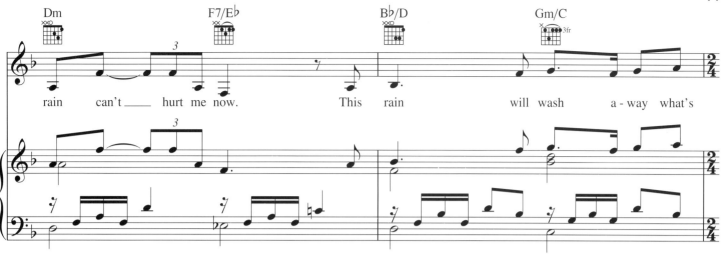

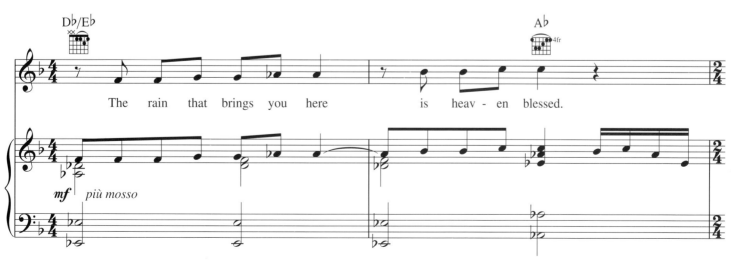

The skies be - gin to clear and I'm at rest. A breath a - way from

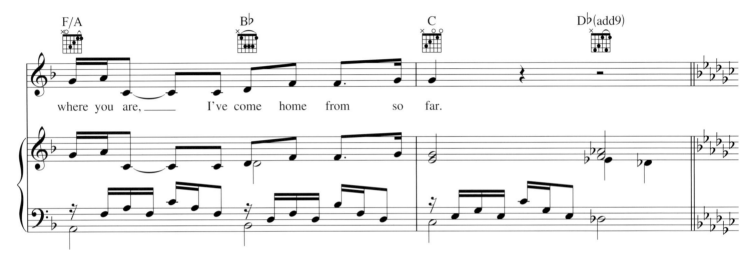

where you are, _____ I've come home from so far.

So don't you fret, M' sieur Mar - ius, ___ I don't feel ___ an - y pain. A

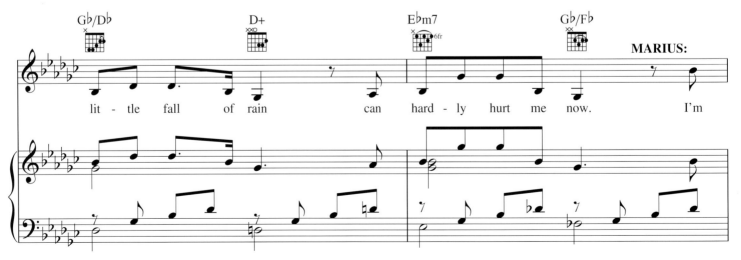

lit - tle fall of rain can hard - ly hurt me now. I'm

here that's all I need to know. And

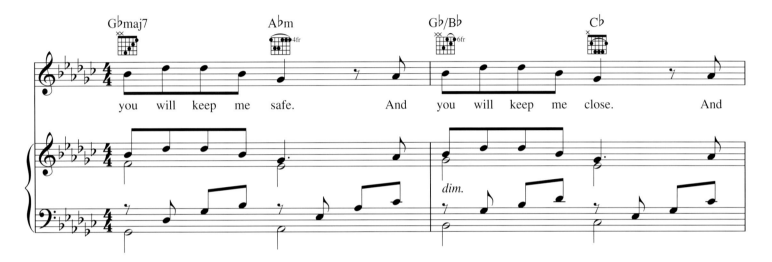

you will keep me safe. And you will keep me close. And

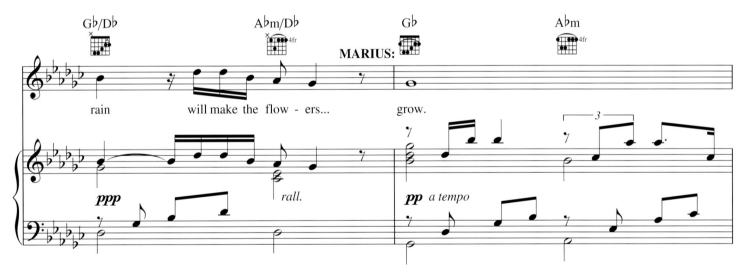

rain will make the flow - ers... grow.

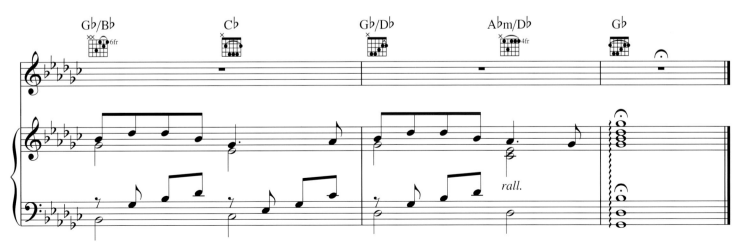

# DRINK WITH ME
## (To Days Gone By)

Music by CLAUDE-MICHEL SCHÖNBERG
Lyrics by HERBERT KRETZMER and ALAIN BOUBLIL

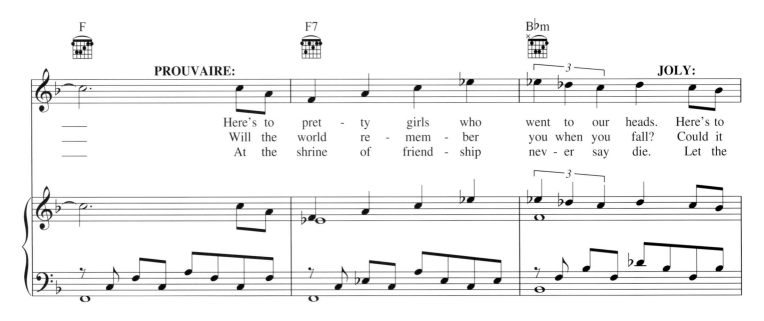

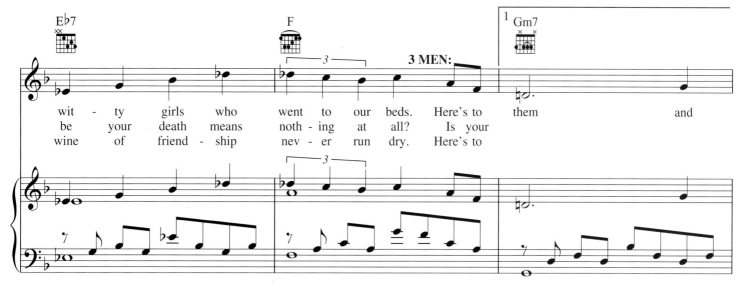

wit - ty girls who went to our beds. Here's to them and
be your death means noth - ing at all? Is your
wine of friend - ship nev - er run dry. Here's to

here's to you! Drink with life just one ___ more lie? ___

**GRANTAIRE:**

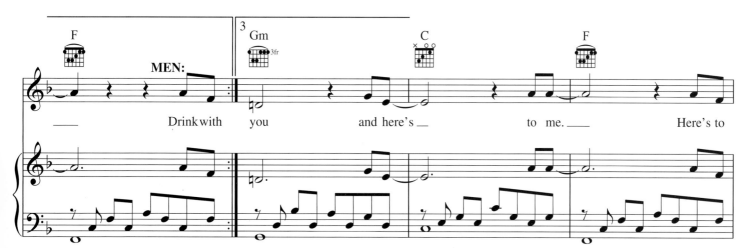

**MEN:**

Drink with you and here's ___ to me. ___ Here's to

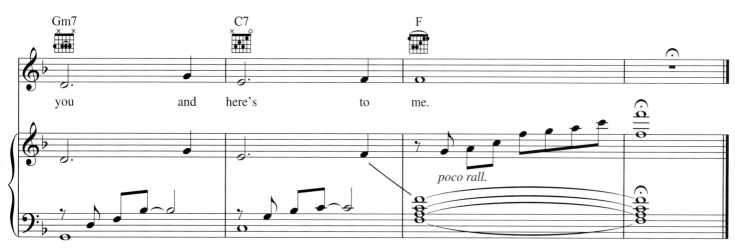

you and here's to me.

*poco rall.*

# BRING HIM HOME

Music by CLAUDE-MICHEL SCHÖNBERG
Lyrics by HERBERT KRETZMER and ALAIN BOUBLIL

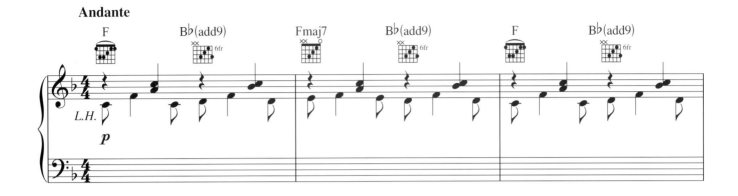

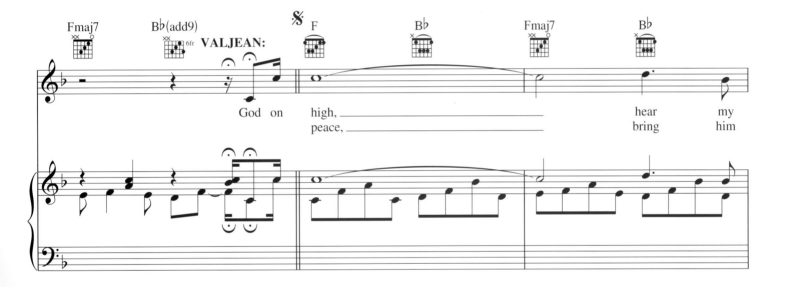

VALJEAN:

God on high, _____ hear my
peace, _____ bring him

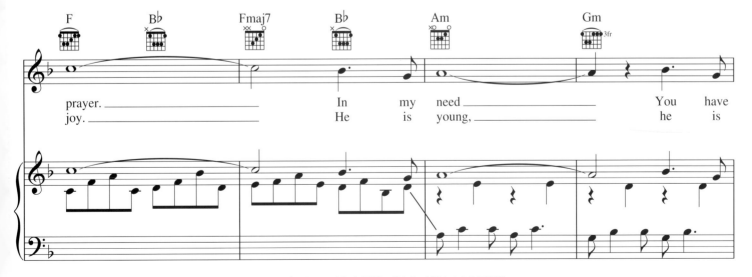

prayer. _____ In my need _____ You have
joy. _____ He is young, _____ he is

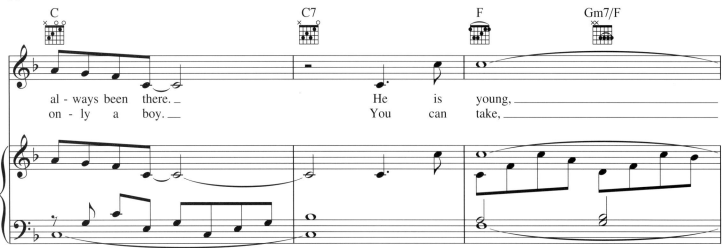

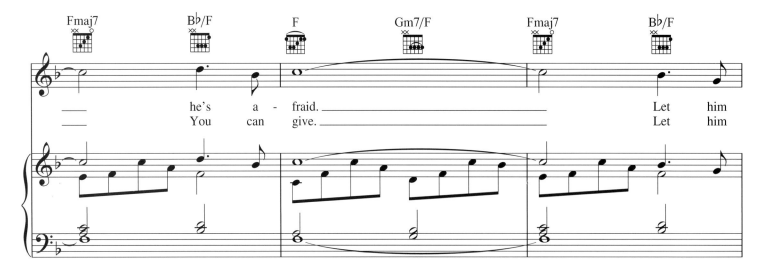

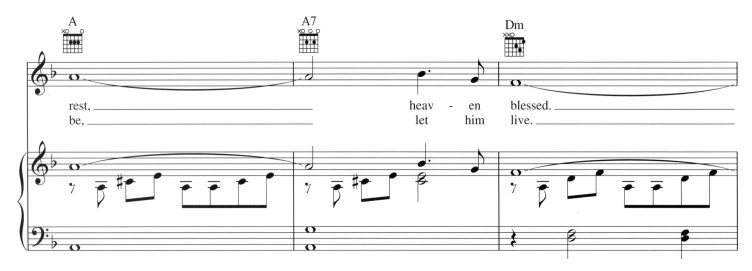

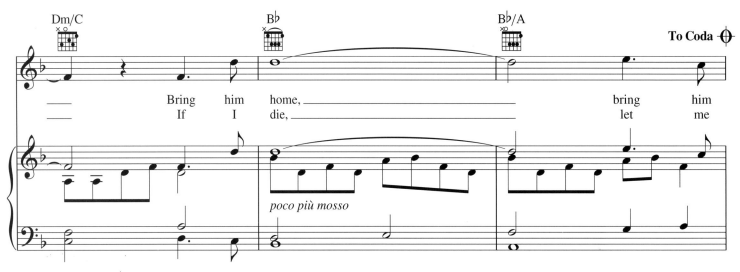

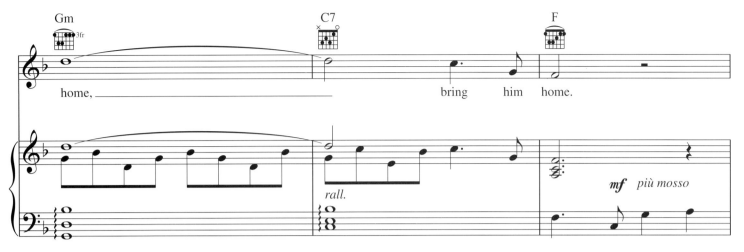

home,_____ bring him home.

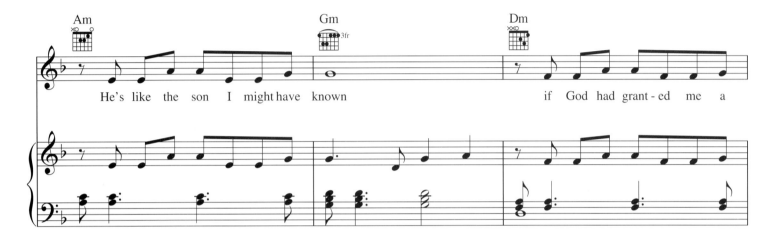

He's like the son I might have known if God had grant-ed me a

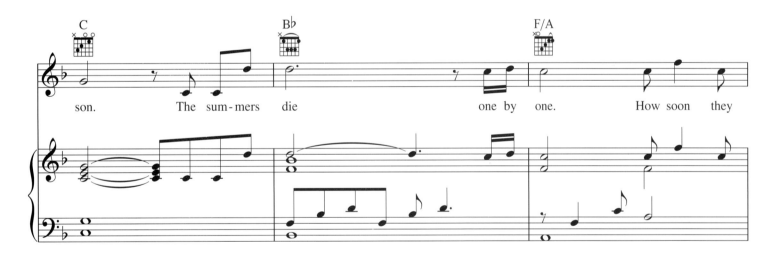

son. The sum-mers die one by one. How soon they

fly on and on. And I am old and will be

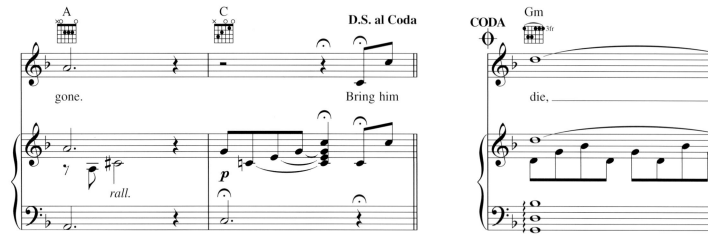

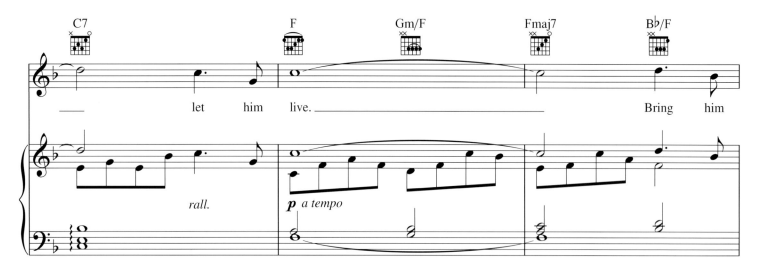

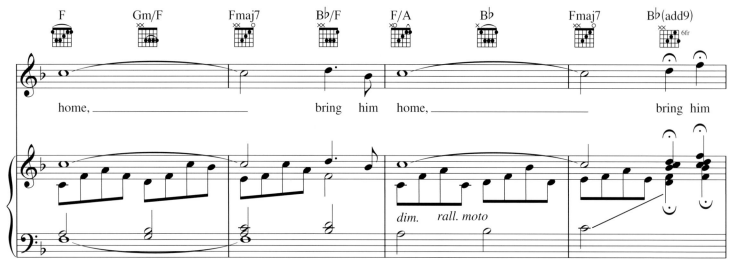

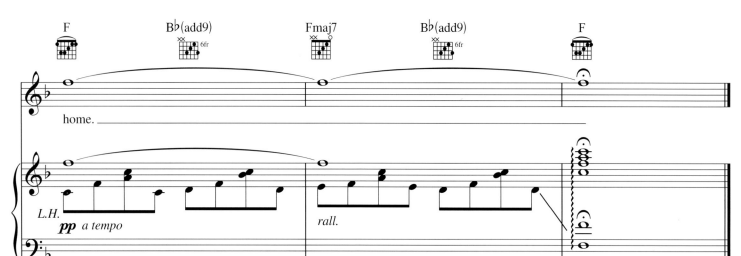

# EMPTY CHAIRS AT EMPTY TABLES

Music by CLAUDE-MICHEL SCHÖNBERG
Lyrics by HERBERT KRETZMER and ALAIN BOUBLIL

gone. Here they talked of rev-o-lu-tion. _____ Here it was they lit the

flame. _____ Here they sang a-bout to-mor-row, and to-

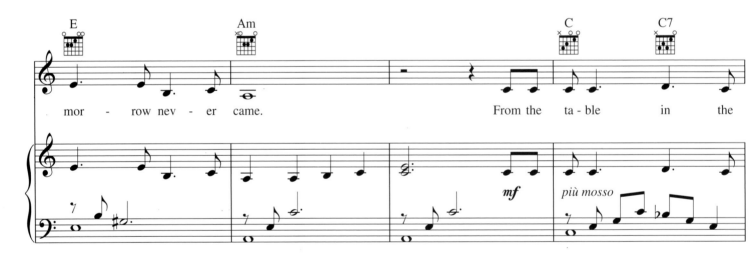

mor-row nev-er came. From the ta-ble in the

cor-ner they could see a world re-born. __ And they

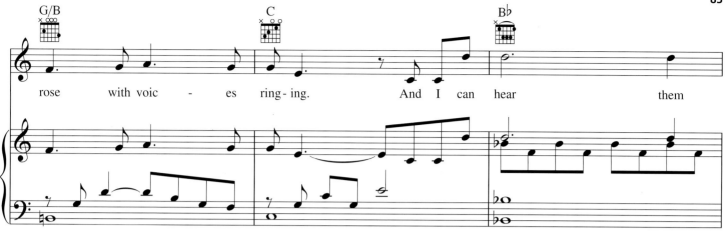

rose with voic - es ring - ing. And I can hear them

now. The ver - y words that they had sung be -

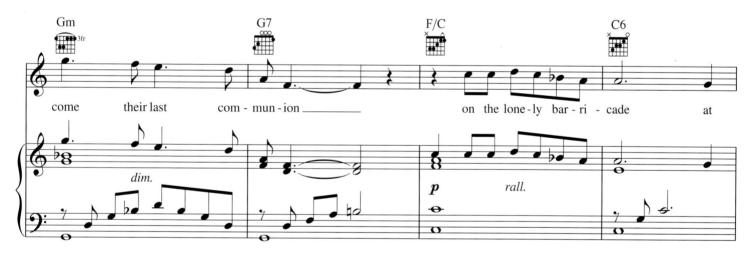

come their last com - mun - ion _____ on the lone - ly bar - ri - cade at

dawn. Oh my friends, my friends, for - give me _____

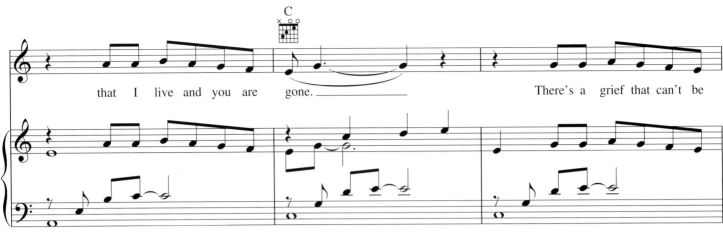

that I live and you are gone. _____ There's a grief that can't be

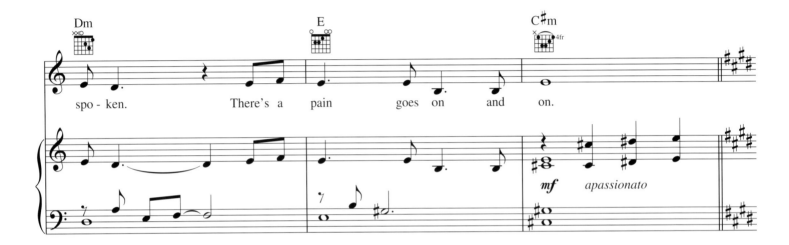

spo - ken. There's a pain goes on and on.

Phan-tom fac - es at the win - dow, _____ phan-tom shad - ows on the

floor. _____ Emp - ty chairs at emp - ty ta - bles where my

friends will meet no more. Oh, my friends, my friends, don't

ask me _____ what your sac - ri - fice was for. _____

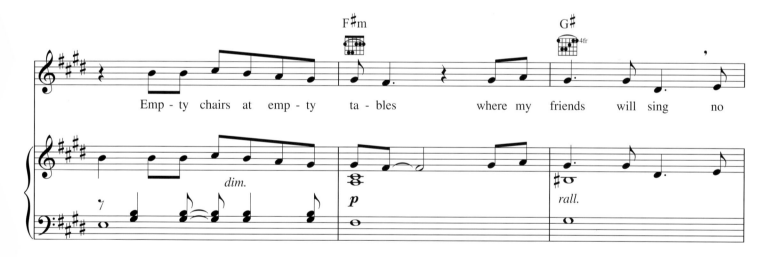

Emp - ty chairs at emp - ty ta - bles where my friends will sing no

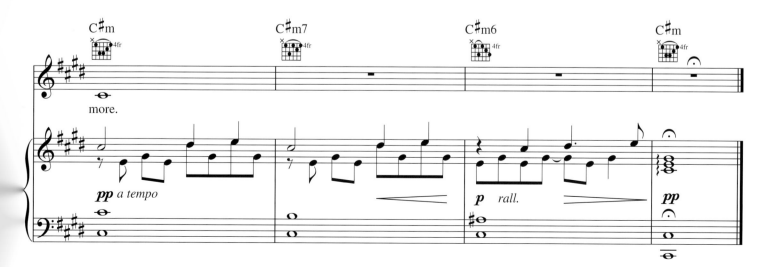

more.

# THE WORLD'S LONGEST-RUNNING MUSICAL

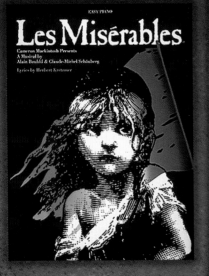

## ALSO AVAILABLE FROM HAL LEONARD